ITIL® Foundation Essentials – ITIL 4 Edition

The ultimate revision guide

ITIL® Foundation Essentials - ITIL 4 Edition

The ultimate revision guide

CLAIRE AGUTTER

IT Governance Publishing

IT Governance Publishing Ltd
Unit 3, Clive Court
Bartholomew's Walk
Cambridgeshire Business Park
Ely, Cambridgeshire
CB7 4EA
United Kingdom
www.itgovernancepublishing.co.uk

© Claire Agutter 2012, 2019.

The author has asserted the rights of the author under the Copyright, Designs and Patents Act, 1988, to be identified as the author of this work.

First published in the United Kingdom in 2012 by IT Governance Publishing

ISBN 978-1-84928-399-1

Second edition published in the United Kingdom in 2019 by IT Governance Publishing

ISBN 978-1-78778-117-7

ABOUT THE AUTHOR

Claire Agutter is a service management trainer, consultant and author. In 2017 and 2018 she was recognised as an HDI Top 25 Thought Leader and was part of the team that won itSMF UK's 2017 Thought Leadership Award. Claire is the host of the popular ITSM Crowd hangouts, and chief architect for VeriSM. Claire is the director of ITSM Zone, which provides online IT service management training, and Scopism, a content and consulting organisation.

After providing training to thousands of successful Foundation delegates, she has condensed the ITIL 4 key concepts necessary to pass the Foundation exam into this guide.

CONTENTS

Introduction 1
Chapter 1: Key concepts of service management 3
   Value 3
   Service management 3
   Organisation 4
   Co-creation 4
Chapter 2: Service management roles 7
   Service provider 7
   Stakeholder 7
   Service relationship 8
   Service consumer 8
Chapter 3: All about services 11
   Products and services 11
   Outputs and outcomes 12
   Cost and risk 14
   Utility and warranty 14
Chapter 4: Service relationships 17
   Service offerings 17
   Service relationships 18
   The service relationship model 20
Chapter 5: Guiding principles 23
   Guiding principle 1: Focus on value 25
   Guiding principle 2: Start where you are 26
   Guiding principle 3: Progress iteratively with
   feedback 27
   Guiding principle 4: Collaborate and promote
   visibility 28
   Guiding principle 5: Think and work holistically 29
   Guiding principle 6: Keep it simple and practical 30

Guiding principle 7: Optimise and automate............. 31
Chapter 6: The four dimensions of service management **33**
Dimension 1: Organisations and people.................... 35
Dimension 2: Information and technology................ 36
Dimension 3: Partners and suppliers 38
Dimension 4: Value streams and processes............... 41
Chapter 7: The Service Value System **45**
Chapter 8: The Service Value Chain **49**
Activity: Plan.. 51
Activity: Improve 52
Activity: Engage 52
Activity: Design and transition................................. 52
Activity: Obtain/build.. 53
Activity: Deliver and support 53
Chapter 9: ITIL Practices.. 55
Practice purposes and key terms............................... 56
Chapter 10: Practices in depth 61
Continual improvement 61
Change control.. 65
Incident management.. 67
Service request management 68
The service desk 69
Problem management 71
Service level management 73
Chapter 11: The ITIL Foundation Exam................... 77
Further reading 79

INTRODUCTION

Welcome to this book. This guide distils the key facts that you need to prepare for a successful ITIL® 4 Foundation exam.

This guide is an ideal revision aid for anyone preparing for their ITIL 4 Foundation exam and is fully aligned with the latest syllabus.

Unless stated otherwise, all quotations are from *ITIL® Foundation, ITIL 4 edition.*

CHAPTER 1: KEY CONCEPTS OF SERVICE MANAGEMENT

This chapter includes:

- Definition of value
- Definition of service management
- Definition of organisation
- How value is co-created
- How organisations collaborate with consumers and suppliers to co-create value

Value

Products and services need to add value to consumers to be successful. Value is *"the perceived benefits, usefulness and importance of something."*

Service management

Service management is *"a set of specialized organizational capabilities for enabling value for customers in the form of services."*

An organisation can only develop these specialised organisational capabilities when it understands:

- The nature of value
- The nature and scope of the stakeholders involved
- How value creation is enabled through services

Organisation

Organisations facilitate value creation. *"An organization is a person or a group of people that has its own functions with responsibilities, authorities, and relationships to achieve its objectives."*

An organisation could be:

- A single person
- A team (within a larger organisation)
- A legal entity (a company, or a charity)
- A government department or public sector body
- A collection of legal entities and teams

Historically, some organisations did not listen to their customers. They saw their relationship with customers as being:

- One-directional
- Distant
- Without feedback

In fact, value is the outcome of a bi-directional relationship. Value is co-created.

Co-creation

Co-creation focuses on customer experience and interactive relationships. It encourages active customer involvement. Organisations need to collaborate with their consumers as well as the suppliers that help them offer valuable services. Each product and service is part of a web of service relationships. Most organisations act as a customer and a service provider as part of service delivery: buying and selling or consuming and supplying services and service elements.

CHAPTER 2: SERVICE MANAGEMENT ROLES

This chapter defines:

- Service provider
- Stakeholder
- Service relationship
- Consumer:
  - Customer
  - User
  - Sponsor
- Examples of value

Service provider

The organisation providing a service is a service provider. A service provider can be part of the same organisation as a consumer (for example, an IT department offering services to a sales team) or an external organisation (for example, a software solutions provider selling to customers).

A service provider must understand who its customers or consumers are, and which other stakeholders are part of its wider service relationships.

Stakeholder

A stakeholder is *"a person or organization that has an interest or involvement in an organization, product, service, practice, or other entity."*

Service relationship

A service relationship is *"a co-operation between a service provider and a service consumer. Service relationships include service provision, service consumption, and service relationship management."*

Service consumer

The service consumer is the person or organisation that is receiving a service. Most organisations will act as service providers and service consumers as part of normal service delivery (for example: as a consumer they buy components to build a service they provide as a service provider). Consumer is a broad term that includes customer, user and sponsor.

Customer	*"A person who defines the requirements for a service and takes responsibility for the outcomes of service consumption."*
User	*"A person who uses services."*
Sponsor	*"A person who authorizes budget for service consumption."*

One individual might act as the customer, the user and the sponsor for a service (for example, an individual who enters into a contract to have a mobile phone fulfils all of these roles). In other situations, the roles are held by separate people (for example, a purchasing department procures mobile phones for staff in a sales team).

Defining roles clearly supports:

- Better communication
- Better relationships
- Better stakeholder management

Roles can have different and conflicting expectations about value, what is an essential requirement, and how much they are prepared to pay.

Different stakeholders receive different types of value.

Stakeholder	Value example
Service consumer	Receives benefits, optimises costs and risks.
Service provider	Funding or loyalty from consumers, further business development, reputation enhancement.
Service provider employees	Job satisfaction, financial and non-financial rewards, personal development.
Society and community	Employment, taxes, corporate social responsibility initiatives.
Charity organisations	Financial and non-financial contributions.
Shareholders	Financial benefits, such as dividends.

CHAPTER 3: ALL ABOUT SERVICES

This chapter defines:

- Products and services
- Utility
- Warranty
- Output
- Outcome
- Risk

Products and services

The services an organisation provides are based on one or more products. Products are created from configurations of the resources an organisation has access to. Resources include:

- People
- Information
- Technology
- Value streams
- Processes
- Suppliers
- Partners

"A service is a means of enabling value co-creation, by facilitating outcomes that customers want to achieve, without the customer having to manage specific costs and risks."

"A product is a configuration of an organization's resources designed to offer value for a consumer."

Service providers need to consider the following areas to assess whether or not they are delivering something that will support value co-creation:

- Cost
- Risk
- Outputs
- Outcomes
- Utility
- Warranty

Outputs and outcomes

A service provider organisation produces outputs, which help its consumers to achieve their desired outcomes. This is where co-creation is important; without input or activity from the consumer, no value is created.

"An output is a tangible or intangible deliverable of an activity."

"An outcome is a result for a stakeholder enabled by one or more outputs."

Value is created when a service has more positive than negative effects. For example, it might cost a consumer money to pay for an externally provided email service, but it reduces the amount of money they spend on internal resources and transfers the risks associated with hardware failure to another organisation. Figure 1 shows this balance

Figure 1: Achieving value: outcomes, costs and risks[1]

between the costs and risks removed or introduced by a service.

The service provider needs to understand the costs of service provision to make sure they are within set budgetary constraints and the organisation is profitable, where relevant. For example, public sector organisations might be required to meet budget targets rather than generate a profit.

_____

[1] *ITIL® Foundation, ITIL 4 edition*, figure 2.2.

Cost and risk

Cost is *"the amount of money spent on a specific activity or resource."*

Risk is *"a possible event that could cause harm or loss or make it difficult to achieve objectives. Risk can also be defined as uncertainty of outcome and can be used in the context of measuring the probability of positive outcomes as well as negative outcomes."*

Service providers manage the detail of risk on behalf of the consumer. The consumer participates in risk reduction by helping to define the service, and what it needs to do.

Utility and warranty

Service providers assess the utility and warranty of a service to check it will create value.

- Utility describes what the service does (fit for purpose)
- Warranty describes how the service performs (fit for use)

"Utility is the functionality offered by a product or service to meet a particular need." This describes what the service does, and whether it is fit for purpose. A service can provide utility by removing constraints from the consumer or supporting their performance, or both.

"Warranty is the assurance that a product or service will meet agreed requirements." Warranty describes how a service performs and whether it is fit for use. Warranty covers areas like availability, capacity, security and

continuity; the service must meet the levels required by the consumer.

Cost, risk, utility and warranty all provide a picture of a service's viability.

CHAPTER 4: SERVICE RELATIONSHIPS

This chapter explains service relationships including:

- Service offerings
- Service relationship management
- Service provision
- Service consumption

Service offerings

"A service offering is a description of one or more services, designed to address the needs of a target consumer group. A service offering may include goods, access to resources, and service actions."

Goods	With goods, ownership is transferred to the consumer – for example, buying a car. The consumer takes responsibility for future use of the goods.
Access to resources	With access to resources, ownership is not transferred to the consumer – for example, renting a car. Access is granted or licensed under agreed terms and conditions – for example, the consumer might agree not to drive more than 10,000 miles per year.

Service actions	Service actions are performed by the provider to address a consumer need – for example, roadside assistance if a car breaks down. They are performed according to the agreement with the consumer – for example, paying extra to have guaranteed assistance within one hour.

The consumer groups that a service is offered to may be part of the same organisation as the service provider, or they might be external to the service provider. Service providers can offer the same product in different ways to different consumer groups; for example, short-term or long-term car leases, or leases with a right-to-buy at the end of the lease.

Service relationships

"A service relationship is a cooperation between a service provider and a service consumer. Service relationships include service provision, service consumption, and service relationship management."

Service provision	*"Activities performed by an organization to provide services. This includes management of resources configured to deliver the service, access to these resources for users, fulfilment of agreed service actions, service performance management and*

	continual improvement. It may also include the supply of goods."
Service consumption	*"Activities performed by an organization to consume services. This includes the management of the consumer's resources needed to use the service, service use actions performed by users, and may include receiving (acquiring) goods."*
Service relationship management	*"This includes joint activities performed by a service provider and a service consumer to ensure continual value co-creation based on agreed and available service offerings."*

Figure 2 shows a generic representation of a service.

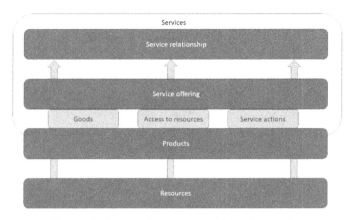

Figure 2: A generic representation of a service

The service relationship model

Figure 3[2] shows the service relationship model.

Services delivered by Organization A create or modify resources within Organization B. Organization B can then use these resources to provide services to its own consumers. For example, laptop manufacturer B buys chips from Organization A so it can sell its laptops to Organization C, which gives them to its consultants.

This diagram shows a supply and consumption chain, but remember that for most organisations, supply and consumption is a more complex network of relationships.

---

[2] *ITIL Foundation, ITIL 4 edition*, figure 2.1.

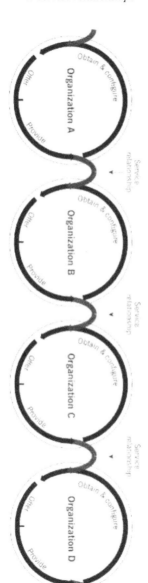

Figure 3: The service relationship model

CHAPTER 5: GUIDING PRINCIPLES

A guiding principle is a *"recommendation that guides an organization in all circumstances."*

Many things change in day-to-day operations:

- Goals
- Key staff
- Strategies
- Types of work
- Management structure

The principles remain constant, no matter what else changes. Using guiding principles allows organisations to integrate multiple ways of working and management methods within service management. For example, some organisations follow a waterfall way of working, and others use methods like Agile and DevOps. The principles allow different ways of working to be used, while making sure appropriate outcomes are delivered.

Waterfall	*"Waterfall is a development approach that is linear and sequential with distinct objectives for each phase of development."*
Agile	*"Agile is an umbrella term for a collection of frameworks and techniques that together enable teams and individuals to work in a way that is typified by collaboration, prioritization, iterative and incremental*

	delivery and timeboxing. There are specific methods (or frameworks) that are classed as Agile, such as Scrum, Lean and Kanban."
DevOps	*"DevOps is an organizational culture that aims to improve the flow of value to customers. DevOps focuses on culture, automation, Lean, measurement and sharing (CALMS)."*

The guiding principles should encourage and support continual improvement. They apply across the whole organisation at all levels – all staff should be aware of them. In each situation, staff and organisations should consider their principles and what is applicable. Not all principles are relevant in every situation, but they all need to be reviewed on each occasion to assess if they are appropriate.

The ITIL guiding principles are:

- Focus on value
- Start where you are
- Progress iteratively with feedback
- Collaborate and promote visibility
- Think and work holistically
- Keep it simple and practical
- Optimise and automate

Guiding principle 1: Focus on value

"Everything the organization does should link back, directly or indirectly, to value for itself, its customers, and other stakeholders."

Services that offer value are attractive to customers. Services must also offer value to the service provider organisation. Focus on value can include:

- Understanding and identifying the service consumer
- Understanding the consumer's perspective of value
- Mapping value to intended outcomes, and understanding these can change over time
- Understanding the customer experience (CX) and/or user experience (UX)

Customer experience (CX)	Customer experience is *"the sum of functional and emotional interactions with a service and service provider as perceived by a service consumer."*
User experience (UX)	User experience is the experience of interacting with a product or service focusing on usability and aesthetics (e.g., user interface, touch and feel of the interaction, graphics, content, features, ease of use...). Sometimes known as the digital experience (DX).[3]

---

[3] *VeriSM: Unwrapped and Applied.*

Service providers need to know:

- Why consumers use services
- What the services help them to do (outcomes)
- How services help them achieve goals
- The cost to the consumer
- The risks for the consumer

To successfully apply this principle, service providers need to consider:

- How consumers use each service
- How to encourage all of their staff to focus on value
- How to maintain a focus on value in day-to-day operations, not just as an improvement project
- How to embed focus on value in every single improvement initiative

Guiding principle 2: Start where you are

Change can be an evolution or a revolution. Revolution is more disruptive and can have unforeseen negative consequences. Before making any change or improvement, it's important to assess the current position and see if anything can be reused or built on.

Start where you are can include:

- Assess where you are
- Observe current services, processes and methods

- Use measurements to analyse what is being observed; remember that measuring can affect the results of what is measured

To successfully apply this principle, service providers need to consider:

- Being as objective as possible about what currently exists
- Assessing whether current practices and services can/should be replicated or expanded
- Using risk management skills during decision making
- Recognising that sometimes nothing from the current state can be reused

Guiding principle 3: Progress iteratively with feedback

"Resist the temptation to do everything at once. Even huge initiatives must be accomplished iteratively. By organizing work into smaller, manageable sections that can be executed and completed in a timely manner, the focus on each effort will be sharper and easier to maintain."

Feedback can help service providers to understand:

- End user and customer perception of value
- The efficiency and effectiveness of their services and value chain
- The effectiveness of governance and management controls

- The interfaces between the organisation and suppliers and partners
- Demand for products and services
- Improvement opportunities, risks and issues

Working iteratively and using feedback helps service providers to be:

- More flexible
- More responsive to changing requirements
- More able to identify and respond to failures
- More quality focused

To successfully apply this principle, service providers need to consider:

- Comprehending the whole, but doing something; start small
- Seeking feedback because the ecosystem is always changing
- Going fast, which doesn't mean work is incomplete; iterations may be small, but they are still producing results

Guiding principle 4: Collaborate and promote visibility

Collaboration can be viewed as working together towards a shared goal. It can help to remove silos within organisations, allowing everyone to work together more effectively. Collaboration can happen anywhere – inside and outside of the organisation (for example: with other internal teams, or with external suppliers).

Promoting visibility makes work more transparent. This helps everyone to:

- Understand what is a priority
- Balance improvement work and daily work
- Understand the flow of work
- Understand where there are bottlenecks
- Identify where time, resources and money are being wasted

To successfully apply this principle, service providers need to consider:

- Collaboration does not mean consensus; it's not essential that everyone agrees, but everyone must understand why decisions are made
- Communicating to match the audience: different stakeholder groups will need a different message and communication type
- Looking for visible data to support good decisions

Guiding principle 5: Think and work holistically

"No service, practice, process, department or supplier stands alone. The outputs that the organization delivers to itself, its customers and other stakeholders will suffer unless it works in an integrated way to handle its activities as a whole, rather than separate parts. All the

organization's activities should be focused on the delivery of value."

The complexity of the system will affect how this principle is applied; higher complexity can create challenges.

To successfully apply this principle, service providers need to consider:

- Collaboration supports holistic thinking and working
- Supporting holistic working with automation
- Identifying patterns in the needs of, and interactions between, system elements to help identify the holistic viewpoint

Guiding principle 6: Keep it simple and practical

"Always use the minimum number of steps to accomplish an objective. Outcome-based thinking should be used to produce practical solutions that deliver valuable outcomes."

Processes and services are designed to meet the majority of consumers' needs. Every exception cannot be designed for. It is better to create rules that can be used to handle exceptions when necessary.

To successfully apply this principle, service providers need to consider:

- Ensuring value comes from every activity
- Simplicity can be more challenging to create than complexity
- Doing fewer things and doing them better

- Respecting people's time; don't make them do unnecessary work
- Simplicity can support quick wins
- Processes or services that are easy to understand are more likely to be used

Guiding principle 7: Optimise and automate

Optimisation means *"to make something as effective and useful as it needs to be. Before an activity can be effectively automated, it should be optimized to whatever degree is possible and reasonable"*. Automation typically refers to *"the use of technology to perform a step or series of steps correctly and consistently with limited or no human intervention."*

Optimisation can include:

- Understanding and agreeing the context for optimisation
- Assessing the current state
- Agreeing the future state and prioritising, focusing on simplification and value
- Ensuring stakeholder engagement and commitment
- Executing improvements iteratively
- Continually monitoring the impact of optimisation

Automation can include:

- Focusing on simplification and optimisation before automation

- Defining metrics to measure impact and value
- Using complementary guiding principles:
  - Progress iteratively with feedback
  - Keep it simple and practical
  - Focus on value
  - Start where you are

CHAPTER 6: THE FOUR DIMENSIONS OF SERVICE MANAGEMENT

The four dimensions are:

1. Organisations and people
2. Information and technology
3. Partners and suppliers
4. Value streams and processes

The four dimensions of service management are relevant to all elements of the Service Value System. Failing to consider all of the four dimensions can lead to services that offer poor quality or efficiency or may even mean services aren't delivered at all. The four dimensions can overlap and interact in unpredictable ways. The four dimensions must be considered for every service. Figure 4 shows the four dimensions.

The four dimensions of service management

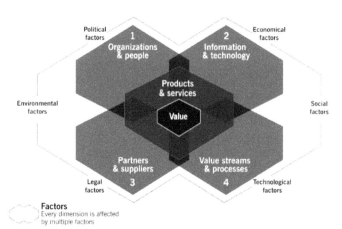

Figure 4: The four dimensions of service management[4]

The factors on the edge of the figure can all affect or constrain any of the four dimensions. For example, legal factors might limit which country an organisation can store information in. Any factor can affect any dimension. The factors are based on PESTLE, which is a framework used to assess macro-environmental factors. Not considering any of the four dimensions can lead to reduced value or no value at all. For example, an organisation might focus too much on technology and neglect the people who are going to use it, leading to no value being delivered.

---

[4] *ITIL Foundation, ITIL 4 edition*, figure 3.1.

Dimension 1: Organisations and people

"The complexity of organizations is growing, and it is important to ensure that the way an organization is structured and managed, as well as its roles, responsibilities, and systems of authority and communication, is well defined and supports its overall strategy and operating model."

The scope of organisations and people includes:

- Formal organisational structures
- Culture
- Required staffing and competencies (skills)
- Roles and responsibilities

Culture is an essential part of an organisation's success or failure. Considerations include:

- Trust
- Transparency
- Collaboration and shared values
- Leadership who champion values
- Coordination

Some of the areas that organisations have to consider as part of this dimension include:

- Management and leadership styles
- Updating skills and competencies
- Communication and collaboration

- Broad knowledge plus deep specialisation of employees (for example, building T-shaped people)
- Common objectives
- Breaking down silos

Dimension 2: Information and technology

Organisations need to consider:

- What information is managed by the services
- What supporting information and knowledge are needed to deliver and manage the services
- How the information and knowledge assets will be protected, managed, archived and disposed of

Technology that supports IT services includes:

- IT architecture
- Databases
- Blockchain
- Cognitive computing
- Applications (including mobile applications)
- Communication systems
- Artificial intelligence
- Cloud computing

Technology that supports IT service management includes:

- Workflow management
- Communication systems

- Inventory systems
- Mobile platforms
- Cloud solutions
- Knowledge bases
- Analytical tools
- Remote collaboration
- Artificial intelligence
- Machine learning

Many IT-enabled services rely on effective information management to deliver value (for example: loyalty schemes, cloud storage for photos). Information management includes the areas shown in the table below.

Availability	*"The ability of an IT service or other configuration item to perform its agreed function when required."*
Reliability	*"The ability of a product, service or other configuration item to perform its intended function for a specified period of time or number of cycles."*
Accessibility	Accessibility includes making sure information is only available to those who should have access to it, and also designing for all consumers, including those with disabilities.

Timeliness	Is information available at an appropriate or useful time?
Accuracy	Is information accurate?
Relevance	Is information relevant?

Dimension 3: Partners and suppliers

"The partners and suppliers dimension encompasses an organization's relationships with other organizations that are involved in the design, development, deployment, delivery, support and/or continual improvement of services. It also incorporates contracts and other agreements between the organization and its partners or suppliers."

The scope of the partners and suppliers dimension includes:

- Service provider/service consumer relationships
- An organisation's partner and supplier strategy
- Factors that influence supplier strategies
- Service integration and management (SIAM)

Supplier and partner relationships range from simple, commodity services to complex partnerships with shared goals and risks. Very few organisations operate completely independently and use no services from other organisations.

Service integration and management (SIAM)	As organisations rely on more and more suppliers, it can prove challenging to manage them, particularly when things go wrong. SIAM is a management methodology that uses a service integrator role to coordinate service relationships across all suppliers. Service integration and management might be carried out by staff within the organisation or by an external organisation.

Figure 5 shows how the service integrator role sits between service providers and the commissioning (customer) organisation.

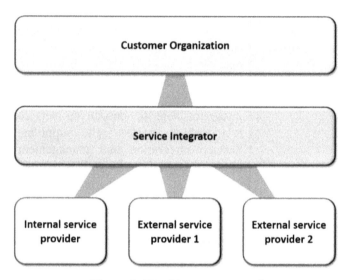

Figure 5: The SIAM ecosystem[5]

The following table explains the factors that can affect an organisation's supplier strategy.

Strategic focus	Some organisations value self-sufficiency, whereas others prefer to outsource non-core work.
Corporate culture	Cultural bias can influence sourcing decisions, perhaps based on past bad experiences.

---

[5] *Service Integration and Management Foundation Body of Knowledge*, Scopism Limited, 2017.

Resource scarcity	Some resources and skills are hard to find, forcing an organisation to source them externally.
Cost concerns	It may be cheaper to source services externally – for example, using shared resources to provide 24x7 support.
Subject matter expertise	Suppliers can bring deep expertise that the organisation cannot build internally.
External constraints	Legislation and regulation can affect sourcing decisions.
Demand patterns	Organisations might use external suppliers to help them cope with spikes in demand – for example, using seasonal staff to provide extra support during holiday periods.

Dimension 4: Value streams and processes

"Applied to the organization and its Service Value System, the value streams and processes dimension is concerned with how the various parts of the organization work in an integrated and coordinated way to enable value creation through products and services. The dimension focuses on what activities the organization undertakes and how they are organized, as well as how the organization ensures that it is enabling value creation for all stakeholders efficiently and effectively."

Value streams and processes define the activities, workflows, controls and procedures needed to achieve agreed objectives.

The scope of this dimension includes:

- Activities the organisation undertakes
- How activities are organised
- How value creation is ensured for all stakeholders efficiently and effectively

An organisation needs to understand its value streams to improve its overall performance. A value stream is *"a series of steps an organization undertakes to create and deliver products and services to consumers."*

Organisations will:

- Examine work and map value streams
- Analyse streams and steps to identify waste
- Eliminate waste
- Identify improvements
- Continually optimise value streams

The key message for processes is:

"A process is a set of activities that transform inputs into outputs. Processes describe what is done to accomplish an objective, and well-defined processes can improve productivity within and across organizations. They are usually detailed in procedures, which outline who is involved in the process, and work instructions, which explain how they are carried out."

A process is a set of interrelated or interacting activities that transforms inputs into outputs. Processes are designed to accomplish a specific objective. Figure 6 shows a simple example:

Figure 6: A simple process

Value streams and processes for products and services help to define:

- The generic delivery model for the service, and how the service works
- The value streams involved in delivering the agreed outputs of the service
- Who, or what, performs the required service actions

CHAPTER 7: THE SERVICE VALUE SYSTEM

The ITIL Service Value System (SVS) is *"a model representing how all the components and activities of an organization work together to facilitate value creation."*

It includes:

- Guiding principles
- Governance
- Service value chain
- Practices
- Continual improvement
- Inputs and outcomes

"The ITIL SVS describes how all the components and activities of an organization work together as a system to enable value creation. Each organization's SVS has interfaces with other organizations, forming an ecosystem that can in turn facilitate value for those organizations, their customers, and their stakeholders."

Figure 7 shows the SVS.

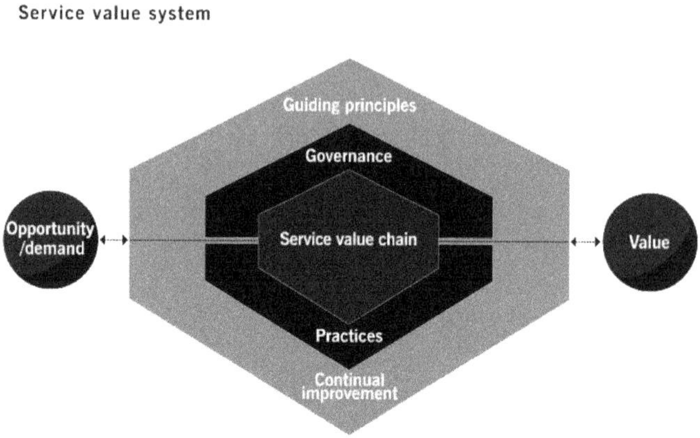

Service value system

Figure 7: The ITIL Service Value System[6]

The table below further explains the SVS:

Opportunity/ demand	Opportunities represent options or possibilities to add value for stakeholders or otherwise improve the organisation. Demand is the need or desire for products and services that originates from internal and external consumers.
Value	The outcome of the SVS is value. The SVS can enable the creation of different types of value for different stakeholders.

[6] *ITIL Foundation, ITIL 4 edition,* figure 4.1.

Guiding principles	The guiding principles are recommendations that can guide an organisation in all circumstances, regardless of changes in goals, strategies, types of work or management structure.
Governance	Governance is the means by which an organisation is directed and controlled. Governance activities include evaluate, direct and monitor.
Service value chain	The service value chain is a set of interconnected activities that an organisation performs in order to deliver a valuable product or service to its consumers and to facilitate value realisation.
Practices	The ITIL practices are sets of organisational resources designed for performing work or accomplishing an objective.
Continual improvement	Continual improvement is a recurring organisational activity performed at all levels to ensure that an organisation's performance is always aligned to changing stakeholder expectations.

CHAPTER 8: THE SERVICE VALUE CHAIN

The value chain is the central element of the Service Value System. It is an operating model that outlines the key activities required to respond to demand and facilitate value through products and services. The activities in the value chain are:

- Plan
- Improve
- Engage
- Design and transition
- Obtain/build
- Deliver and support

Figure 8 shows the service value chain.

Service value chain

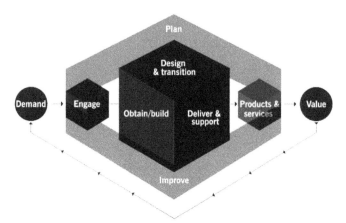

Figure 8: The ITIL service value chain[7]

Activities in the chain don't necessarily happen in a linear flow. Activities may happen in parallel, be repeated, or occur as a series of iterations. Different products, services and consumers will lead to different streams of work and different routes through the value chain. For example, developing a new application will be different from amending an existing one. These are an organisation's value streams: combinations of practices and value chain activities that lead to value.

Each value chain activity relies on inputs and creates outputs for other activities. The activities are all interconnected. Skipping an activity, or spending less time

---

[7] *ITIL Foundation, ITIL 4 edition*, figure 4.2.

on it than is needed, will impact the whole value chain as other activities will not get the inputs they need.

There are some key points to remember about the service value chain activities:

- All interactions with parties external to the service provider are performed via ENGAGE.
- All new resources are obtained through OBTAIN/BUILD.
- All planning takes place in the PLAN activity.
- Component, product and service creation, modification, delivery, maintenance and support is performed in an integrated way by the DESIGN AND TRANSITION, OBTAIN/BUILD, and DELIVERY AND SUPPORT activities.
- Products and services, demand and value are SVS components, not value chain activities.

Activity: Plan

"The purpose of the plan value chain activity is to ensure a shared understanding of the vision, current status, and improvement direction for all four dimensions and all products and services across the organization."

Information inputs into the PLAN activity are used to create key outputs including improvement opportunities (for IMPROVE) and contract agreements (for ENGAGE).

Activity: Improve

"The purpose of the improve value chain activity is to ensure continual improvement of products, services and practices across all value chain activities and the four dimensions of service management."

DELIVER AND SUPPORT provide service performance information and ENGAGE provides information about service elements provided externally. Outputs include improvement initiatives, status reports and service performance information for DESIGN AND TRANSITION.

Activity: Engage

"The purpose of the engage value chain activity is to provide a good understanding of stakeholder needs, transparency, and continual engagement and good relationships with all stakeholders."

ENGAGE provides oversight of requests and feedback from customers, as well as incidents to help identify IMPROVE opportunities.

Activity: Design and transition

"The purpose of the design and transition value chain activity is to ensure that products and services continually meet stakeholder expectations for quality, costs and time to market."

This activity receives portfolio decisions as an input, as well as information about components provided by suppliers from ENGAGE. This activity will create (among other outputs) requirements and specifications that are passed to OBTAIN/BUILD and contract requirements that are passed to ENGAGE.

Activity: Obtain/build

"The purpose of the obtain/build value chain activity is to ensure that service components are available when and where they are needed and meet agreed specifications."

Organisations need to decide whether to create products and services themselves, or to use external resources, or a combination.

Activity: Deliver and support

"The purpose of the deliver and support value chain activity is to ensure that services are delivered and supported according to agreed specifications and stakeholders' expectations."

This activity will receive new or updated services, including service components from OBTAIN/BUILD and user support tasks from IMPROVE. The outputs will include the new or updated service being offered to users.

CHAPTER 9: ITIL PRACTICES

"A practice is a set of organizational resources designed for performing work or accomplishing an objective."

Each ITIL practice supports multiple service value chain activities. Practices are made up of resources from the four dimensions of service management:

1. Organisations and people
2. Information and technology
3. Partners and suppliers
4. Value streams and processes

The ITIL Service Value System includes 34 practices:

- 14 general management practices
- 17 service management practices
- 3 technical management practices

This publication only addresses practices covered in the ITIL 4 Foundation syllabus.

General management practice	These practices are adopted and adapted for service management from business management.
Service management practice	These practices have been developed in service management and IT service management.

Technical management practice	These practices originated in technology management and have been adapted for service management.

Practice purposes and key terms

The ITIL 4 Foundation syllabus requires you to know the purpose of 15 ITIL practices. For some of these 15, you also need to know key terms, and there are 7 practices that are studied in more depth.

Information security management

This is a general management practice.

"The purpose of the information security management practice is to protect the information needed by the organization to conduct its business. This includes understanding and managing risks to the confidentiality, integrity, and availability of information, as well as other aspects of information security such as authentication (ensuring someone is who they claim to be) and non-repudiation (ensuring that someone can't deny that they took an action)."

Relationship management

This is a general management practice.

"The purpose of the relationship management practice is to establish and nurture the links between the organization and its stakeholders at strategic and tactical levels. It includes the identification, analysis, monitoring and

continual improvement of relationships with and between stakeholders."

Supplier management

This is a general management practice.

"The purpose of the supplier management practice is to ensure that the organization's suppliers and their performances are managed appropriately to support the seamless provision of quality products and services. This includes creating closer, more collaborative relationships with key suppliers to uncover and realize new value and reduce the risk of failure."

IT asset management

This is a service management practice.

"The purpose of the IT asset management practice is to plan and manage the full lifecycle of all IT assets, to help the organization:

- *Maximize value*
- *Control costs*
- *Manage risks*
- *Support decision making about purchase, re-use, retirement and disposal of assets*
- *Meet regulatory and contractual requirements."*

An IT asset is *"any financially valuable component that can contribute to the delivery of an IT product or service."*

Monitoring and event management

This is a service management practice.

"The purpose of the monitoring and event management practice is to systematically observe services and service components, and record and report selected changes of state identified as events. This practice identifies and prioritizes infrastructure, services, business processes, and information security events, and establishes the appropriate response to those events, including responding to conditions that could lead to potential faults or incidents."

An event is *"any change of state that has significance for the management of a service or other configuration item. Events are typically recognized through notifications created by an IT service, configuration item or monitoring tool."*

Release management

This is a service management practice.

"The purpose of the release management practice is to make new and changed services and features available for use."

A release is *"a version of a service or other configuration item, or a collection of configuration items, that is made available for use."*

Service configuration management

This is a service management practice.

"The purpose of the service configuration management practice is to ensure that accurate and reliable information about the configuration of services, and the configuration items that support them, is available when and where it is needed. This includes information on how configuration items are configured and the relationships between them."

A configuration item (CI) is *"any component that needs to be managed in order to deliver an IT service."*

Deployment management

This is a technical management practice.

"The purpose of the deployment management practice is to move new or changed hardware, software, documentation, processes, or any other component to live environments. It may also be involved in deploying components to other environments for testing or staging."

CHAPTER 10: PRACTICES IN DEPTH

The ITIL 4 Foundation syllabus also requires 7 practices to be studied in depth. These are covered in this chapter.

Continual improvement

Continual improvement is a general management practice.

"The purpose of the continual improvement practice is to align the organization's practices and services with changing business needs through the ongoing improvement of products, services and practices, or any element involved in the management of products and services."

Continual improvement records improvement opportunities in the continual improvement register (CIR). This can be a written document, spreadsheet or database. It allows improvement ideas to be logged, prioritised, tracked and managed. Some ideas are never implemented due to cost or timing issues.

Each idea is:

- Documented
- Assessed
- Prioritised
- Implemented if appropriate
- Reviewed

Continual improvement needs to happen at all levels of the organisation:

- Leaders must embed continual improvement and build a culture that allows it to thrive.
- The continual improvement practice will have ownership of continual improvement and will cheerlead it across the organisation.
- All staff will participate in continual improvement; it must be seen as part of everyone's role.
- Suppliers and partners should also contribute to improvement initiatives; this is often included in their contracts, which describe how improvements are reported and measured.

Continual improvement activities include:

- Encouraging continual improvement across the organisation
- Securing time and budget for continual improvement
- Identifying and logging improvement opportunities
- Assessing and prioritising improvement opportunities
- Making business cases for improvement action
- Planning and implementing improvements
- Measuring and evaluating improvement results
- Coordinating improvement activities across the organisation

There are many different methods and techniques that continual improvement can use. It's important to select the right technique for the right situation, rather than try to use them all at once. Methods and techniques include:

- Lean
- Multi-phase project
- Maturity assessments
- DevOps
- Balanced scorecard
- Incremental or agile improvements
- Quick wins
- SWOT analysis

The continual improvement model

Figure 9 shows the continual improvement model:

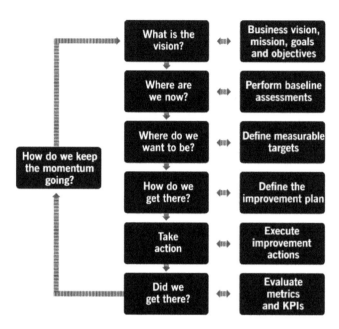

Figure 9: The continual improvement model[8]

The continual improvement model provides a high-level guide for improvement initiatives. It allows organisations to focus on customer value and link back to their vision. Following the steps in the model allows work to be divided into manageable sections, so small goals are achieved and momentum is maintained. Improvement is not a one-off activity: as one improvement initiative completes, another begins.

---

[8] *ITIL Foundation, ITIL 4 edition*, figure 4.3.

Change control

Change control is a service management practice.

"The purpose of the change control practice is to maximize the number of successful service and product changes by ensuring that risks have been properly assessed, authorizing changes to proceed, and managing the change schedule."

"A change is the addition, modification, or removal of anything that could have a direct or indirect effect on IT services."

The person or group who authorises a change is referred to in ITIL as the 'change authority'. Change authority may be decentralised in organisations working at high speed and in agile environments, meaning peer review is more important and becomes an indicator of high performance. The change schedule is used to help plan changes, assist in communication, avoid conflicts and assign resources.

Change control must balance delivering benefits through successful changes and protecting live service from harmful changes.

The following table shows the change types:

Standard change	Standard changes are low-risk, preauthorised changes. They are well understood and documented so they can be implemented without additional authorisation. An example of a standard change could be giving a new starter access to a piece of approved software.

Normal change	Normal changes need to be scheduled, assessed and authorised via the organisation's defined process. Lower-risk changes will need less scrutiny than high-risk changes. Many organisations have tools in place that manage change request workflows, automating the process where it makes sense to do so.
Emergency change	Emergency changes need to be implemented as soon as possible, perhaps in response to an issue or a security breach. They are assessed and authorised when possible, but some steps (e.g. testing) might be left out if the level of urgency justifies it. There may be a separate change authority for emergency changes.

Each organisation will define its own scope for change control. This often includes:

- IT infrastructure
- Applications
- Documentation
- Processes
- Supplier relationships
- Any other relevant areas

Incident management

Incident management is a service management practice.

"The purpose of the incident management practice is to minimize the negative impact of incidents by restoring normal service operation as quickly as possible."

An incident is *"an unplanned interruption to or reduction in the quality of a service."*

Incidents need to be logged, prioritised, and resolved within agreed timescales. They might be escalated to a support team for resolution, depending on the product or service affected and how quickly the resolution is required. Incident management needs to include quality, timely updates to the affected user(s) which requires a high level of collaboration between teams. The incident management practice activities include:

- Design the incident management practice: the practice has to react differently to different incident types, depending on their impact. Major incidents and security incidents might require special handling.
- Prioritise incidents: incidents with the highest impact need to be resolved first. Classifications and timescales are agreed with consumers.
- Use an incident management tool: have a tool for logging and managing incidents. The tool may provide links to changes, known errors and knowledge articles. It may also provide incident matching and links to problems.

Swarming

Some organisations use an incident management technique called swarming. A group of stakeholders work together until it becomes clear who is best placed to continue with the incident. Collaboration like this supports information sharing and provides learning opportunities within the teams.

Service request management

Service request management is a service management practice.

"The purpose of the service request management practice is to support the agreed quality of a service by handling all pre-defined, user-initiated service requests in an effective and user-friendly manner."

A service request is *"a request from a user or a user's authorized representative that initiates a service action which has been agreed as a normal part of service delivery."*

Service requests are different from incidents because they are part of normal service delivery. Nothing has failed. They are handled using pre-defined and pre-agreed procedures, liaising with change control where necessary.

Common types of service request include:

- Request for a service delivery action
- Request for information
- Request for provision of a resource or service
- Request for access to a resource or service

- Feedback, compliments and complaints

Successful service request management relies on these considerations:

- Service request management should be automated and standardised as much as possible
- Continual improvement should be applied to service request management
- Policies should be used to allow requests to be fulfilled with appropriate authorisation
- User expectations should be clearly set
- Requests that are actually incidents or changes need to be redirected to the appropriate practice

Service requests can have simple or complex workflows. The steps in the workflows should be well-known and proven. The service provider will agree fulfilment times and provide clear status communication to users. Some service requests can be fulfilled via self-service; for example, requesting a new piece of software or access to a printer.

The service desk

The service desk is a service management practice.

"The purpose of the service desk practice is to capture demand for incident resolution and service requests. It should also be the entry point and single point of contact for the service provider with all of its users."

The service desk will capture and funnel demand:

- Acknowledge: the user needs to know that their contact has been received; for example, issues reported via email could receive an auto-acknowledgement.
- Classify: classification helps the service desk to understand what they are dealing with and how important it is.
- Own: ownership ensures no issue or request gets 'lost' between teams or systems.
- Act: resolving things to the user's satisfaction.

Possible service desk channels include:

- Telephone
- Service portals
- Mobile applications
- Live chat and chatbots
- Email
- Walk-in
- Text messages and social media messaging
- Public and private discussion forums

Service desks may be centralised or virtual:

- Virtual: agents can work from multiple locations, using technology to allow them to collaborate.
- Centralised: the service desk is a team working in a single location.

Some service desk staff are very technical, others are less technical and work more closely with technical teams within the organisation. Service desk staff skills include:

- Empathy
- Emotional intelligence
- Effective communication
- Customer service skills
- Understanding of business priority, incident analysis and prioritisation

Technologies that support service desks include:

- Intelligent telephony systems
- Workforce management/resource planning systems
- Call recording and quality control
- Dashboard and monitoring tools
- Workflow systems
- Knowledge base
- Remote access tools
- Configuration management systems

Problem management

Problem management is a service management practice.

"The purpose of the problem management practice is to reduce the likelihood and impact of incidents by identifying actual and potential causes of incidents and managing workarounds and known errors."

"A problem is a cause, or potential cause, of one or more incidents." Problems require investigation and analysis to identify the causes, develop workarounds, and recommend longer-term resolution to reduce the number and impact of future incidents.

"A workaround is a solution that reduces or eliminates the impact of an incident or problem for which a full resolution is not yet available. Some workarounds reduce the likelihood of incidents." Workarounds are documented in problem records, and then reviewed and improved as problem analysis progresses. A workaround can be as simple as asking a user to reboot a PC, or more complex.

"A known error is a problem that has been analyzed but not yet resolved." Known errors are documented and made available to other practices, for example the service desk.

Figure 10 shows the three phases of problem management:

Figure 10: The phases of problem management[9]

Problem identification activities identify and log problems.

They include:

- Trend analysis of data including incident records
- Detection of recurring issues
- Identifying whether major incidents might recur

---

[9] *ITIL Foundation, ITIL 4 edition,* figure 5.23.

- Working with suppliers and partners
- Analysing information from developers, testing and project teams

Problem control activities include:

- Problem analysis, prioritisation and management based on risk
- Documenting workarounds
- Documenting known errors

Error control activities include:

- Identifying potential permanent solutions
- Ongoing management and reassessment of known errors
- Ongoing management and improvement of workarounds

Problem management interfaces with other practices including change control and incident management as part of its role.

Service level management

Service level management is a service management practice.

"The purpose of the service level management practice is to set clear business-based targets for service levels, and to ensure that delivery of services is properly assessed, monitored, and managed against those targets."

A service level is *"one or more metrics that define expected or achieved service quality."*

A service level agreement is *"a documented agreement between a service provider and a customer that identifies both services required and the expected level of service."*

Service level agreements (SLAs) are used to measure the service performance from the customer's point of view.

Successful SLAs need to:

- Relate to a defined service so the scope is clear
- Relate to outcomes, not just operational metrics like '99% availability'
- Reflect agreement between customer and service provider
- Be simple to read and understand

Service level management provides end-to-end visibility of an organisation's services:

- It establishes a shared view of services and target service levels
- It collects, analyses, stores and reports on relevant metrics
- It performs service reviews and identifies improvement opportunities
- It captures and reports on service issues

Key skills for service level management include:

- Relationship management

- Business liaison
- Business analysis
- Supplier management

Service level management will collect information from:

- Business metrics, which measure business activities such as making a sale or processing an invoice
- Operational metrics, which help to build a picture of overall performance and whether outcomes are being met
- Customer feedback, including surveys and defined business-related measures
- Customer engagement, including initial conversations and listening, discovery and information capture, measurement and ongoing process discussions, and asking simple open-ended questions

CHAPTER 11: THE ITIL FOUNDATION EXAM

The ITIL Foundation exam is:

- 40 multiple-choice questions
- 60 minutes (extra time may be allowed for non-native English speakers if no translated paper is available)
- Pass mark of 26/40 or 65%
- No negative marking
- Closed book

FURTHER READING

IT Governance Publishing (ITGP) is the world's leading publisher for governance and compliance. Our industry-leading pocket guides, books, training resources and toolkits are written by real-world practitioners and thought leaders. They are used globally by audiences of all levels, from students to C-suite executives.

Our high-quality publications cover all IT governance, risk and compliance frameworks and are available in a range of formats. This ensures our customers can access the information they need in the way they need it.

Our other publications about ITSM include:

- *Practical IT Service Management - A concise guide for busy executives*
  www.itgovernancepublishing.co.uk/product/practical-it-service-management

- *Ten Steps to ITSM Success - A Practitioner's Guide to Enterprise IT Transformation*
  www.itgovernancepublishing.co.uk/product/ten-steps-to-itsm-success

- *ITSM, ITIL & ISO20000 Implementation Toolkit*
  www.itgovernancepublishing.co.uk/product/itsm-itil-iso20000-implementation-toolkit

For more information on ITGP and branded publishing services, and to view our full list of publications, visit *www.itgovernancepublishing.co.uk*.

To receive regular updates from ITGP, including information on new publications in your area(s) of interest, sign up for our newsletter at *www.itgovernancepublishing.co.uk/topic/newsletter*.

Branded publishing

Through our branded publishing service, you can customise ITGP publications with your company's branding.

Find out more at *www.itgovernancepublishing.co.uk/topic/branded-publishing-services*.

Related services

ITGP is part of GRC International Group, which offers a comprehensive range of complementary products and services to help organisations meet their objectives.

For a full range of resources on ITIL visit *www.itgovernance.co.uk/itil*.

Training services

The IT Governance training programme is built on our extensive practical experience designing and implementing management systems based on ISO standards, best practice and regulations.

Our courses help attendees develop practical skills and comply with contractual and regulatory requirements. They also support career development via recognised qualifications.

Learn more about our training courses in ITIL and view the full course catalogue at *www.itgovernance.co.uk/training*.

Professional services and consultancy

We are a leading global consultancy of IT governance, risk management and compliance solutions. We advise businesses around the world on their most critical issues and present cost-saving and risk-reducing solutions based on international best practice and frameworks.

We offer a wide range of delivery methods to suit all budgets, timescales and preferred project approaches.

Find out how our consultancy services can help your organisation at *www.itgovernance.co.uk/consulting*.

Industry news

Want to stay up to date with the latest developments and resources in the IT governance and compliance market? Subscribe to our Daily Sentinel newsletter and we will send you mobile-friendly emails with fresh news and features about your preferred areas of interest, as well as unmissable offers and free resources to help you successfully start your projects: *www.itgovernance.co.uk/daily-sentinel*.

CPSIA information can be obtained
at www.ICGtesting.com
Printed in the USA
BVHW040158190520
579944BV00015B/604

9 781787 781177